The Gallbladder Diet
(US Edition)

MAIN DISHES

EASY LOW-FAT RECIPES FOR A HEALTHY LIFE
AFTER GALLBLADDER REMOVAL SURGERY

by Iris Pilzer

CONTENTS

Tasty Vegetables

Asparagus with jamón serrano	10
Curry with lentils	14
Eggplants with couscous	14
Grilled asparagus	8
Green asparagus sunny side up	8
Home-made fries	16
Mexican sweet corn	16
Oven-baked asparagus	8
Ratatouille	12
Tarte flambée with tomatoes	18
Tomatoes with beans	18
Vegetarian chili	12
Wild asparagus	10

Delish Pasta

Broccoli casserole	28
Fettuccine de Paris	22
Fried Spätzle with dried tomatoes	26
Oven-baked ravioli	20
Pasta with chestnuts	24
Pasta with zucchini and eggplant	22
Spaghetti bolognese	28
Spaghetti with spicy tomato sauce	20
Vegetable bolognese	24
Vegetable lasagna	26

Yummy Rice

Coconut milk rice with raspberry puree	34
Zucchini risotto	30
Kentucky stew	36
Mushroom risotto	32
Rice curry with beans and peas	34
Risotto (basic recipe)	30
Tomato risotto	32
Vegetable rice	36

Juicy Meat

Andalusian-style chicken fillet	38
Chicken breast with garlic and lemon	38
Chili con carne	42
Fast goulash	42
Greek-style stir-fry	40
Oriental stir-fry	40

Fresh Fisch

Couscous with fennel and shrimps	46
Fish buns with tartar sauce	44
Fish sticks with mashed peas	44
Fish with couscous	48
French-style one-pan fish	48
Neapolitan cod	46

NOVEMBER 2017, MY LIFE WAS OVER.

I had an awful pain in my stomach area. The only thing I wanted to do was to cower in my bed and die. My doctor's diagnosis: gall- stones. Lots of them. Which had shut down my life for the past 6 month without me knowing what was wrong. I had surgery late November. A laparoscopic cholecystectomy. In layperson's terms: my gallbladder was removed. And two days later I was discharged from hospital with the sound advice that I should eat low-fat food from now on.

Of course, this suggestion was most helpful (please note my sarcasm). Until then, fat was an important part of my diet. The human body needs fat. And women in particular need a certain amount of fat every day to stay healthy. And now the doctors and nurses were telling me that, suddenly, I should stop eating fat?

O.K., I found out pretty quickly that too much fat isn't good for me. My liver still continues to produce bile, but I don't have a gallbladder anymore to store bile for the times when I eat a lot of fat. And, as it turned out, this had a rather unpleasant effect on my digestion.

On the plus side: I really like to cook. So this wasn't the end for me. I started a process of trial and error to find out what my body could tolerate – and what my body wouldn't tolerate. I simply took the dishes that I had liked before my surgery and changed them. Mostly, I cut high-fat ingredients and tried to find substitutes. Also, I tested how much fat my body could tolerate in one meal, and I adapted my recipes to that. Now I have a small collection of recipes tailor-made for people who had their gallbladder removed.

Have fun and a good time when trying my recipes. I would love to hear from you what you think about my recipes – in a review or via e-mail.

To a healthy, low-fat diet.

Iris Pilzer

THE WAY OF LIFE WITHOUT A GALLBLADDER:

Eat a lot of fibers. They prevent your body from forming new gallstones. You can find lots of fibers in oatmeal, most vegetables, crispbread and bread made from rye flour.

Eat 5 to 6 small meals a day to make things easier for your digestive system.

Try to find out how much fat your body can tolerate in one meal. Then try to eat exactly this amount of fat at each meal.

Don't worry if your meal has more fat than your body can stomach: take an artichoke capsule or drink a beer with your meal (preferably non- alcoholic beer).

Find out which foods your body can't tolerate. Try to steer clear of these foods in the future. Carefully try foods that cause bloating, such as onions, garlic, legumes, cabbage and kale, cucumbers, and peppers and chilis (including paprika). Spicy dishes might cause your digestive system to rebel.

When you eat out: Ask what's in what you want to order. If you can't tolerate some types of foods, tell them. There's no need to suffer so that others have less work (for which you still have to pay) or aren't offended.

Drink a lot of liquid. Best would be water and tea without sugar. Aim to drink 7 to 9 cups of water a day. And while you're at it, test if you can tolerate carbonated water.

Buy day-old bread. If you can't get hold of any, toast fresh bread for 5 seconds. You might also have a problem with other freshly baked pastries (e.g., yeast dough).

Avoid processed foods. These are often heavily spiced. Fresh food is better for your digestion (and it tastes better!).

Reduce your alcohol intake. Your liver will thank you!

Keep a food log so that you don't lose track of what you should and what you shouldn't eat.

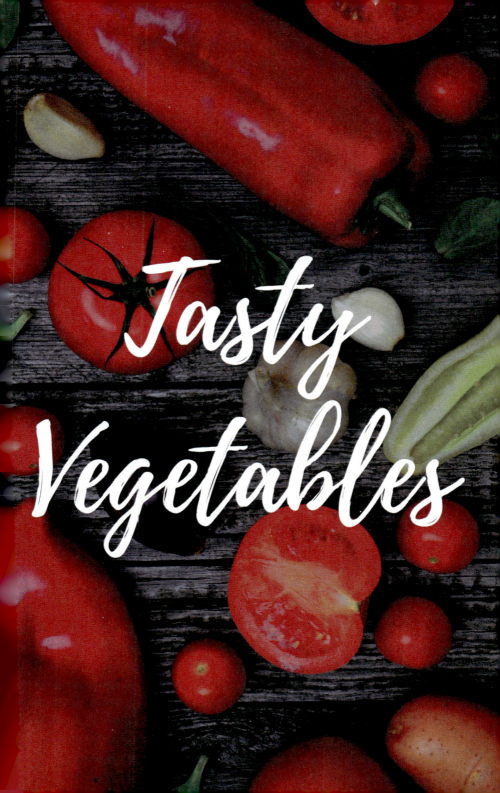

GREEN ASPARAGUS SUNNY SIDE UP

For 2 servings:
1 lb green asparagus • 1 tbsp olive oil • 2 eggs • bread

- Remove the woody ends from your asparagus. Wash and pat dry.
- Bring water to a boil in a pot. Add salt. Boil the asparagus for 2 to 3 minutes or until tender. Remove the asparagus and let it drain.
- In the meantime, heat the oil in a medium-size pan. Crack the eggs into the pan and reduce the heat. Cook the eggs until the whites are done but the yolk is still runny. Serve hot with the asparagus.

OVEN-BAKED ASPARAGUS

For 2 servings:
1 lb asparagus • 1 lb red and yellow cherry tomatoes • 1 small chili • 4 slices of bacon • 2 tbsp oil • ½ lemon • bread

- Preheat the oven to 400 °F.
- Remove the woody ends from the asparagus. Wash and pat dry. Wash and halve the cherry tomatoes. Wash the chili, remove the seeds and finely chop.
- Place the asparagus, the tomatoes and the chili in a large casserole dish. Drizzle with olive oil and lemon juice. Toss well. Drape the bacon on top.
- Place in the oven for 10 to 15 minutes. Turn on the grill of your oven for the last 2 minutes. Serve hot with bread.

GRILLED ASPARAGUS

For 2 servings:
1 lb green asparagus • 1-2 tbsp olive oil • salt, pepper • bread

- Remove the woody ends from your asparagus. Wash and pat dry.
- Fry the asparagus in a griddle pan without adding any fat. Turn once when the asparagus starts to char. The asparagus is done when it has a dark green color.
- Place the asparagus on a plate. Drizzle with olive oil and season well with salt and pepper. Serve hot with bread.

Asparagus with Jamón Serrano

For 2 servings:

1 lb green or purple asparagus • jamón serrano • 2 tbsp olive oil • pepper

To taste and tolerance:

aioli as a dip • bread

- Preheat the oven to 400 °F.
- Sprinkle a baking dish with 1 tbsp of olive oil. Halve the jamón serrano lengthways.
- Remove the woody ends from your asparagus. Wash and pat dry. Wrap each asparagus with one half of the jamón serrano. Place in the baking dish and sprinkle with the rest of the oil. Season well with pepper.
- Bake the asparagus in the preheated oven for 10 minutes. Serve hot with aioli and bread.

Wild asparagus

For 2 servings:

1 lb wild asparagus or green asparagus • 1 egg • 1 tbsp milk • 2 tbsp flour • 3 tbsp olive oil • salt, pepper • bread

- Remove the woody ends from your asparagus. Wash and pat dry. Halve the asparagus so that it cooks more easily (because now it's shorter).
- Bring water to a boil in a pot. Add salt. Boil the asparagus for 2 to 3 minutes or until tender. Remove the asparagus and let it drain.
- In a shallow bowl, whisk the egg with the milk and salt and pepper. Spread the flour on a plate.
- Heat the oil in a large pan. Turn the asparagus in the flour. Then coat in the egg mixture. Place in the hot pan immediately and fry until golden.
- Remove the asparagus from the pan and place on a paper towel. Season with salt and pepper and serve hot with bread.

Ratatouille

For 2 servings:

olive oil • 1 yellow bell pepper • 1 zucchini • 1 eggplant • 1 red onion • 2 cloves of garlic • 1 can (15 oz) canned tomatoes • 1 pinch salt, pepper, sweet paprika • ½ tspn sugar • ½ bunch basil • 1 pre-baked ciabatta bread • 2 oz goat's curd

- Preheat the oven to 440 °F. Prepare the ciabatta according to the instructions on the package.
- Wash the zucchini and the eggplant and roughly chop. Wash the bell pepper, remove the seeds and cut into strips. Peel the onion and cut into eight pieces. Place the vegetables in a casserole dish with 2 tbsp of olive oil and salt and pepper. Roast in the oven until soft.
- Peel the garlic and finely chop. Heat 1 tspn of olive oil in a large pan. Sauté the garlic until soft. Add the canned tomatoes and season well with sweet paprika, salt, pepper and ½ tspn of sugar. Let the sauce simmer on low heat.
- Wash the basil, shake dry and roughly chop. Place the vegetables and the basil in the sauce and stir well. Serve with small pieces of goat's curd.

Vegetarian chili

For 2 servings:

½ cup (8 oz) rice • 1 red onion • ½ chili • ½ tspn cumin • ½ tspn smoked sweet paprika • 1 clove of garlic • 2 tbsp olive oil • 1 bell pepper • 1 can (15 oz) chickpeas • 1 can (15 oz) kidney beans • 1 can (15 oz) canned tomatoes

- Bring 10 fl oz of water to the boil in a small pot. Once boiling, add salt and the rice. Let the rice cook for 10 minutes at low heat, then remove it from the heat and let it rest for another 10 minutes.
- Peel the onion and the garlic. Wash and deseed the bell pepper and the chili. Roughly chop the vegetables.
- Heat the olive oil in a large pot. Add the cumin and the smoked sweet paprika and sauté. Add the onion and the garlic and sweat on a medium heat until soft. Add the bell pepper and the chili and let it cook for 5 minutes.
- Drain the chickpeas and the kidney beans. Place in the pot together with the canned tomatoes. Stir well. Let the chili simmer on a low or medium heat for 10 minutes.

EGGPLANTS WITH COUSCOUS

For 2 servings:

1 large eggplant • olive oil • ½ tspn dried oregano • 1 pinch salt • 1 red onion • 1 clove of garlic • ½ bunch parsley • 1 can (15 oz) canned tomatoes • 1 tbsp capers • 8 pitted green olives • 1 tbsp red wine vinegar • ½ cup (8 oz) couscous

- Wash the eggplant, remove the ends and roughly chop.
- Heat 2 tbsp of olive oil in a large pot. Sear the eggplant together with oregano and salt for 4 to 5 minutes.
- Peel the onion and the garlic and finely chop. Wash the parsley and finely chop the stalks. Add and cook for 1 minute.
- Drain the capers and the olives and add to the eggplants. Drizzle with red wine vinegar. Add the canned tomatoes and squash them roughly. Let the sauce simmer for 15 minutes.
- Prepare the couscous according to the instructions on the package. Add a little parsley.
- Serve with couscous and sprinkle with the rest of the parsley.

CURRY WITH LENTILS

For 2 servings:

1 large onion • 1 clove of garlic • 1 red bell pepper • 1 tbsp rapeseed oil or peanut oil • 1 ½ cup red lentils• 1 can (15 oz) coconut milk • 2 tspn mild red curry paste • 1 naan bread • 4 tbsp low-fat natural yoghurt

- Peel the onion and garlic and finely chop. Wash the bell pepper, remove the seeds and roughly chop.
- Heat the peanut oil in a pot. Sauté the onion, the garlic and the bell pepper until soft.
- Add the lentils and 3 cups of boiling water. Add the coconut milk and the curry paste. Put on a lid and let simmer at a low heat until the lentils are done. Stir occasionally so that the curry won't burn.
- Serve the curry with naan bread and yoghurt.

Home-made fries

For 2 servings:
1 lb potatoes • 2 tbsp olive oil • salt, pepper

- Preheat the oven to 440 °F.
- Wash and peel the potatoes. Cut the potatoes into strips. Place in a bowl and mix with olive oil, salt and pepper.
- Spread baking paper on a baking sheet. Place the potatoes on the baking paper and bake in the oven for 25 minutes.

TIP: This also works well with yams (sweet potatoes).

Mexican sweet corn

For 2 servings:
½ lb low-fat minced meat • 1 can sweet corn • 1 can (15 oz) canned tomatoes • 1 pickled green chili • 1 red bell pepper • 2 tbsp olive oil • salt, pepper • 1 spring onion • tortillas

- Drain the sweet corn. Remove the tomatoes from the can and roughly chop (or squeeze with your fingers). Chop the pickled chili. Deseed the bell pepper, wash and roughly chop.
- Heat the olive oil in a pan. Add the minced meat and stir-fry until it has a nice brown color. Add the vegetables and sauté for 5 minutes. Then add the sweet corn. Season well with salt and pepper.
- Wash the spring onion and cut into rings.
- Heat the tortillas in the oven or in the microwave. Spread the sweet corn and the spring onion rings on the tortillas, roll and serve hot.

TIPS: If you don't want to use canned tomatoes, instead you can peel 2 tomatoes in boiling water and roughly chop. Leave out the minced meat for a vegetarian dish.

Tomatoes with Beans

For 2 servings:
1 lb tomatoes • 1 onion • 2 tbsp oil • ½ lb green beans (frozen) • summer savory, garlic powder, salt, pepper, sugar, thyme • ½ bunch parsley

- Wash the tomatoes, remove the stem and roughly chop. Peel the onion and finely chop.
- Heat the oil in a pan. Add the onion and sauté until soft. Add the beans and stir-fry for 5 minutes.
- Add the tomatoes and the herbs. Let stew for 5 minutes.
- In the meantime wash the parsley, shake dry and roughly chop.
- Sprinkle with parsley and serve hot.

TIP: If you want, you can add bacon to give the dish more taste: cut 4 slices of bacon into thin strips. Fry the bacon in the pan before you add the oil and the onion.

Tarte Flambée with Tomatoes

For 4 servings:
1 package of ready-made pizza dough (or tarte flambée dough if you can get it) • ½ bunch basil • 1 cup of sour cream (7 oz) • salt, pepper • 1 lb yellow and red tomatoes

- Preheat the oven to 400 °F.
- Wash the basil, shake dry and remove the leaves. Blend the leaves with sour cream and season well with salt and pepper.
- Wash the tomatoes, remove the stem and cut into slices. Halve small tomatoes.
- Spread the dough on a baking sheet. Spread the basil mix on the dough. Leave some space for the crust. Add the tomato slices.
- Bake in the oven for 10 to 15 minutes.

Spaghetti with Spicy Tomato Sauce

For 2 servings:

4 slices of bacon • 1 tbsp olive oil • 1 large onion • 2 cloves of garlic • 1 can (15 oz) canned tomatoes • 2 tbsp dried pizza herbs (oregano, thyme, rosemary) • ½ tspn cayenne pepper • 1 pinch each: salt, pepper, sugar • ½ lb spaghetti

- Cut the bacon into fine strips and fry in a large pan.
- Peel the onion and the garlic and finely chop. Add a little olive oil to the bacon, then add the onion and the garlic and fry until soft.
- Bring water to a boil in a large pot. Cook the spaghetti according to the instructions on the package.
- Add the tomatoes to the onion and garlic. Crush larger pieces. Add the herbs and spices. Stir well and let simmer for 15 minutes at a low heat.

TIPS: You can easily leave out the bacon. Then you get a fast vegetarian tomato sauce! By the way, you can also use other types of pasta. And by the way: this sauce isn't made only for spaghetti.

Oven-Baked Ravioli

For 2 servings:

1 can ravioli • 2 tbsp cream • butter • 2 tbsp breadcrumbs • 2 tbsp grated cheese

- Preheat the oven to 440 °F.
- Open the can of ravioli. Carefully stir in the cream.
- Spread a little butter in a baking dish. Place the ravioli in the baking dish.
- Mix the breadcrumbs and the cheese. Scatter on top of the ravioli. Spread some small butter pieces on top.
- Place in the oven and bake until the crust has a nice golden color.

Pasta with Zucchini and Eggplant

For 2 servings:
1 large zucchini • 1 small eggplant • salt, pepper • Herbes de Provence • 2 tbsp olive oil • ½ lb pasta • shaved Parmesan or Grana Padano

- Preheat the oven to 400 °F. Bring water to a boil in a large pot.
- Wash the zucchini and the eggplant and cut into small pieces.
- Place baking paper on a baking sheet and add the vegetables. Drizzle with olive oil and season well. Place in the oven and bake for 15 minutes.
- Cook the pasta according to the instructions on the package.
- Remove the vegetables from the oven. Place on top of the pasta. Drizzle with a little olive oil. If you want, you can add some Parmesan or Grana Padano.

Fettuccine de Paris

For 2 servings:
10 fl oz vegetable stock • ¼ lb mushrooms • 1 clove of garlic • ½ lemon • 1 tspn butter • ½ lb fettuccine • ½ tspn Café de Paris • 4 oz low-fat natural yoghurt • salt, pepper

- Prepare 10 fl oz of vegetable stock. Clean and quarter the mushrooms. Peel the garlic and finely chop. Wash the lemon with hot water, finely grate the peel and squeeze the lemon and retain the juice.
- In a medium-size pot, sauté the mushrooms without butter for 1 to 2 minutes. Add the butter and the garlic and fry for 2 to 3 minutes. Add the vegetable stock. Place the pasta in the pot and let cook until the pasta is al dente.
- Once al dente, add the yoghurt, the Café the Paris, the lemon juice and a pinch of the grated lemon peel. Season well with salt and pepper. Stir carefully and heat once again before serving.

Vegetable Bolognese

For 2 servings:

1.5 oz legumes (beans, lentils, etc.; soaked in cold water for at least 12 hours) • salt, pepper • 1 red onion • 1 clove of garlic • 1 celery stalk • 1 tspn dried rosemary • olive oil • 1 can (15 oz) tomatoes • ½ lb spaghetti • shaved Parmesan

- Prepare and cook the legumes according to the instructions on the packaging.
- Peel the onion and the garlic. Clean the celery. Roughly chop the vegetables.
- Heat 1 tbsp of olive oil in a large pot. Add the vegetables and the rosemary and cook until soft.
- Add the canned tomatoes. Add half a can of water. Bring to a boil and let simmer for 10 minutes at a low heat. Then add the legumes.
- In the meantime, prepare the spaghetti according to the instructions on the package.
- Use a masher to roughly mash the sauce (use a hand blender if you want finer sauce). Season well with salt and pepper and serve with shaved Italian cheese.

Pasta with Chestnuts

For 2 servings:

½ lb pasta • 10 fl oz vegetable stock • 4 oz cooked chestnuts • 1 tspn dried rosemary • ¼ bunch of parsley • ½ lemon • 1 tspn olive oil • 3 oz cream cheese • salt, pepper

- Bring water to a boil in a large pot. Cook the pasta according to the instructions on the package.
- Prepare 10 fl oz of vegetable stock. Wash the parsley, shake dry and finely chop. Wash the lemon with hot water, finely grate the peel and squeeze and retain the juice. Finely chop the chestnuts so that they are almost like flour.
- Heat the olive oil in a small pan. Fry the chestnuts for 2 minutes. Add the vegetable stock and bring to a boil. Reduce the heat and add the lemon peel, the cream cheese and the rosemary. Season well with salt and pepper.
- Place the cooked pasta on a plate. Put the chestnut sauce on top and garnish with parsley. Serve and enjoy!

Vegetable Lasagna

For 2 servings:
1 large carrot • 2 celery stalks • 1 small eggplant • 1 small zucchini • 1 small onion • 1 clove of garlic • 2 tspn olive oil • 6 tbsp sieved tomatoes • salt, pepper • ½ tspn of each: dried thyme, rosemary, basil, oregano • 12 lasagna sheets • low-fat grated cheese

- Wash and clean the vegetables and cut into bite-size pieces. Peel the onion and the garlic and finely chop.
- Preheat the oven to 400 °F.
- Heat the olive oil in a large pot. Sauté the onion and the garlic until soft. Add the carrot pieces and fry for 2 minutes. Add the rest of the vegetables and fry for another 2 minutes.
- Add the sieved tomatoes. Season well with salt, pepper and herbs.
- In a baking dish, layer the lasagna sheets and the vegetables. Finish with a top layer of grated cheese. Bake in the oven for 20 to 30 minutes until golden.

Fried Spätzle with Dried Tomatoes

For 2 servings:
1 lb pre-cooked spätzle (you can also use gnocchi) • ½ tbsp butter • ½ lb cherry tomatoes • a handful of dried tomatoes • 10 fl oz vegetable stock • 1 dash of cream • salt, pepper

- Heat the butter in a large pan. Add the spätzle and stir-fry until golden.
- Wash the cherry tomatoes and cut in half. Finely chop the dried tomatoes. Prepare the vegetable stock.
- Add the tomatoes to the spätzle and fry for 2 to 3 minutes. Add the vegetable stock and fry for another 2 to 3 minutes.
- Season well with a dash of cream and salt and pepper. Serve hot.

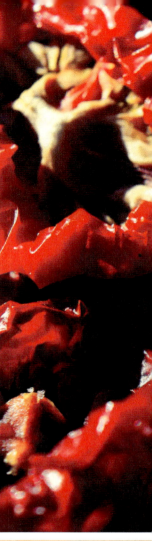

Spaghetti bolognese

For 2 servings:

½ lb spaghetti • salt • 2 onions • ½ tbsp margarine • ½ lb minced meat • 9 fl oz meat broth • 2 tbsp tomato puree • ketchup • pepper, oregano, sweet paprika • shaved Parmesan or Grana Padano

- Bring water to the boil in a pot. Cook the pasta according to the instructions on the packaging.
- Peel the onions and finely chop. Heat the margarine in a large pan. Add the onion and stir-fry until soft.
- Place the minced meat in a second pan. Don't use any fat. Stir-fry until the meat has a nice brown color. Then add the meat to the onions.
- Fill the meat broth into the empty pan and bring to a boil. Add the tomato puree and the ketchup and stir well. Add the broth to the meat and onions. Season well with salt, pepper, oregano and sweet paprika. Let the sauce simmer for 15 minutes.
- Serve the spaghetti with the sauce and shaved Italian cheese.

Broccoli casserole

For 2 servings:

6 oz short pasta • ½ lb frozen broccoli • butter • 3 oz cooked ham • 2 eggs • 3.5 fl oz cream • ¼ tspn salt • 1 pinch nutmeg • pepper • 2 oz grated cheese

- Preheat the oven to 400 °F.
- Bring water to the boil in a pot. Cook the pasta according to the instructions on the packaging.
- Defrost the broccoli with hot water.
- Spread a little butter in a small baking dish. Place the broccoli and the pasta in the baking dish and stir carefully.
- Cut the ham into strips and scatter on the pasta.
- Mix the eggs, the cream, the salt, the nutmeg and the pepper. Spread the mix on the pasta. Scatter grated cheese on top.
- Place the baking dish in the oven and bake for 20 to 30 minutes.

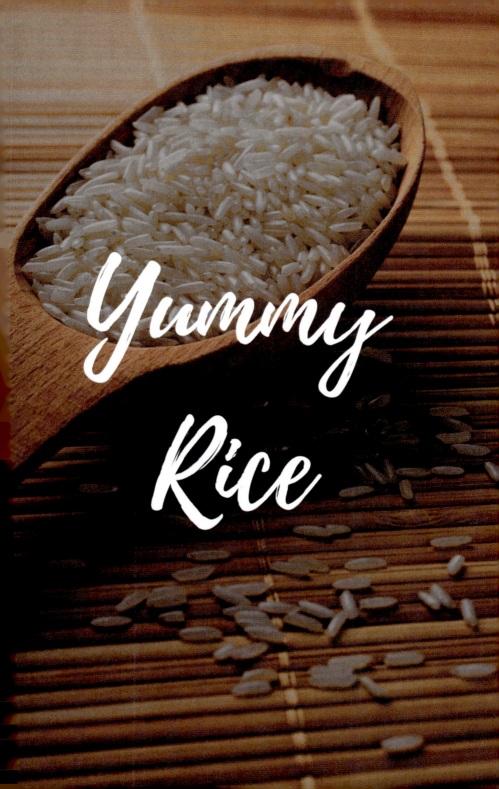

Risotto (Basic Recipe)

For 2 servings:
¾ cup risotto rice • 1 small onion • 1 celery stalk • 1 small clove of garlic • 1 tbsp olive oil • 2 fl oz white wine • 20 fl oz vegetable stock • a handful shaved Grana Padano or Parmesan

- Peel the onion and the garlic and finely chop. Clean and wash the celery stalk and finely chop.
- Heat the olive oil in a pot. Add the onion, the garlic and the celery and fry until soft. Add the rice and fry until transparent.
- In the meantime, prepare the vegetable stock.
- Add white wine or the same amount of vegetable stock. Stir until the liquid is gone, then add another ladle of vegetable stock. Repeat this for 15 to 20 minutes, until the rice is done.
- Remove the pot from the heat. Add the shaved cheese and stir well. Let the risotto rest a little before serving.

Zucchini Risotto

For 2 servings:
¾ cup risotto rice • 1 small onion • 1 celery stalk • 1 small clove of garlic • 1 small zucchini • 1 tbsp olive oil • 2 fl oz white wine • 20 fl oz vegetable stock • a handful shaved Grana Padano or Parmesan • 1 buffalo mozzarella

- Peel the onion and the garlic and finely chop. Clean and wash the celery stalk and finely chop. Wash the zucchini and roughly chop.
- Heat the olive oil in a pot. Add the onion, the garlic and the celery and fry until soft. Add the rice and fry until transparent.
- In the meantime, prepare the vegetable stock and add the zucchini pieces.
- Add white wine or the same amount of vegetable stock. Stir until the liquid is gone, then add another ladle of vegetable stock. Repeat this for 15 to 20 minutes, until the rice is done.
- Remove the pot from the heat. Add Grana Padano and buffalo mozzarella and stir well. Let the risotto rest a little before serving.

Tomato Risotto

For 2 servings:
¾ cup risotto rice • 1 small onion • 1 celery stalk • 1 small clove of garlic • 2 handfuls cherry tomatoes • 2 tbsp olive oil • 2 fl oz white wine • 20 fl oz vegetable stock • 1 handful shaved Grana Padano or Parmesan

- Preheat the oven to 400 °F. Peel the onion and the garlic and finely chop. Clean and wash the celery stalk and finely chop. Wash the cherry tomatoes.
- Place the tomatoes in a baking dish with 1 tbsp of olive oil. Roast in the oven for 10 minutes.
- Heat the olive oil in a pot. Add the onion, the garlic and the celery and fry until soft. Add the rice and fry until transparent.
- Add white wine or the same amount of vegetable stock. Stir until the liquid is gone, then add another ladle of vegetable stock. Repeat this for 15 to 20 minutes, until the rice is done.
- Remove the pot from the heat. Add the cheese and the tomatoes and stir well. Let the risotto rest a little before serving.

Mushroom Risotto

For 2 servings:
¾ cup risotto rice • 1 small onion • 1 celery stalk • 1 small clove of garlic • 2 handfuls mushrooms • 2 tbsp olive oil • 2 fl oz white wine • 20 fl oz vegetable stock • 1 handful shaved Grana Padano or Parmesan

- Preheat the oven to 400 °F. Peel the onion and the garlic and finely chop. Clean and wash the celery stalk and finely chop. Clean the mushrooms.
- Place the mushrooms in a baking dish with 1 tbsp of olive oil. Roast in the oven for 10 minutes.
- Heat the olive oil in a pot. Add the onion, the garlic and the celery and fry until soft. Add the rice and fry until transparent.
- Add white wine or the same amount of vegetable stock. Stir until the liquid is gone, then add another ladle of vegetable stock. Repeat this for 15 to 20 minutes, until the rice is done.
- Remove the pot from the heat. Add the cheese and stir well. Let the risotto rest a little before serving. Top the risotto with mushrooms.

COCONUT MILK RICE WITH RASPBERRY PUREE

For 2 servings:
1 pinch vanilla extract • 1 can (15 oz) low-fat coconut milk • ½ cup short grain white rice • 1 pinch salt • 2 handfuls of frozen raspberries • skim milk

- Remove the raspberries from the freezer so that they can thaw slowly.
- Pour the coconut milk into a pot. Add the vanilla extract and the salt and bring to a boil.
- Add the rice to the coconut milk. Bring to a boil. At a low heat, wait until the coconut milk starts to simmer. Then put on a lid and let the rice simmer for 30 to 40 minutes.
- In the meantime, use a fork to squash the raspberries to a puree.
- Taste the rice after 40 minutes. If the rice is still too firm, add some milk and again bring to a boil.
- Place the rice in 2 bowls. Add the raspberry puree and serve hot.

RICE CURRY WITH BEANS AND PEAS

For 2 servings:
¾ cup basmati rice • 2 pieces of cardamom • ½ cup green beans (frozen) • ½ cup peas (frozen) • 4 spring onions • 3 tomatoes • 1 tbsp peanut oil • 1 can (15 oz) coconut milk • 2 tspn mild red curry paste

- Bring 10 fl oz water to a boil in a pot. Add the rice, the cardamom, the beans and the peas. Put on a lid and cook for 10 minutes on a low heat. Then remove from the heat and let rest for another 10 minutes.
- Clean and wash the spring onions and finely slice. Wash the tomatoes and roughly chop.
- Heat the oil in a large pan. Add the spring onions and sauté for 3 to 4 minutes. Add the tomatoes and stir-fry for 5 minutes.
- Add the coconut milk and the curry paste Stir well. Bring to a boil and serve hot together with the rice.

Vegetable Rice

For 2 servings:
1 bag of boil-in-the-bag rice • 1 small onion • 1 bell pepper • 4 tbsp olive oil • salt, sweet paprika, garlic powder, sugar • 9 fl oz hot water • 1 small can carrots • 1 small can mushrooms • 1 small can peas • 1 tomato • 1 oz grated cheese

- Prepare the rice according to the instructions on the package.
- In the meantime, peel the onion and finely chop. Deseed the bell pepper, wash and roughly chop. Drain the canned vegetables. Roughly chop the carrots and the mushrooms. Wash the tomatoes, remove the stem and roughly chop.
- Heat the oil in a pan. Stir-fry the onion and the bell pepper for 5 minutes until soft. Add the rice and stir-fry for 3 minutes. Season well with salt, paprika, garlic powder and sugar. Continue to stir-fry and add hot water little by little.
- Add the carrots, mushrooms, tomato and the peas. Heat the dish until the vegetables are also hot. Add the grated cheese, stir well and serve hot.

Kentucky Stew

For 2 servings:
½ lb beef • 2 tbsp oil • 1 tbsp tomato puree • 18 fl oz meat broth • 2 small bell peppers • 1 carrot • 1 small leek • 1 cup of rice • ½ can sweet corn • salt, pepper, garlic powder

- Wash the beef and cut into bite-size pieces. Heat the oil in a large pot. Add the beef and stir-fry for 5 minutes.
- Add the tomato puree and the meat broth. Stir well and let simmer on small heat.
- In the meantime, deseed the bell peppers, wash and cut into strips. Peel the carrots and slice. Wash the leek and slice. Add the vegetables to the beef and broth.
- Add the rice and 2 cups of water. Stir well. Cook for 20 minutes until the rice is done.
- Add the sweet corn. Season with salt, pepper and garlic powder. Serve hot.

Andalusian-Style Chicken Fillet

For 2 servings:
2 chicken breast fillets • salt, pepper • 2 tbsp olive oil • 10 pitted black olives • 1 red chili • 3 tomatoes • 3 cloves of garlic • 5 fl oz sherry • bread

- Wash the chicken. Use your hand or a meat tenderizer to flatten the chicken. Season well with salt and pepper. Heat the oil in a medium-size pan. Fry the chicken until golden. Don't worry if the meat burns a little. We need that later.
- Finely slice the olives. Wash the chili, remove the seeds and finely chop. Peel the garlic and finely slice. Wash the tomatoes and roughly chop.
- Add the vegetables. Deglaze with sherry. Use a spatula to remove the burned meat from the bottom of the pan. Put a lid on the pan and cook for 10 minutes.
- Season well with salt and pepper. Serve hot with bread.

Chicken Breast with Garlic and Lemon

For 2 servings:
2 chicken breast fillets (cut into strips) • 1 tbsp olive oil • 1 small onion • 3 cloves of garlic • 1 organic lemon • 2 tbsp chopped parsley • salt, pepper • baguette

- Peel the onion and the garlic and finely chop.
- Heat the olive oil in a large pan. Sauté the onion until transparent. Then add the garlic and sauté for 30 seconds.
- Add the chicken strips and stir-fry for 5 to 10 minutes at medium heat.
- In the meantime, peel several strips of the zest of 2 lemons using a speed-peeler. Finely grate the rest of the peel and squeeze the juice into a small bowl.
- Add the grated lemon peel and the lemon juice. Carefully loosen the brown stuff at the bottom of the pan. Add the parsley and stir carefully. Season well with salt and pepper.
- Garnish with lemon zest and serve hot with baguette.

Oriental Stir-Fry

For 2 servings:
¾ cup rice • ½ lb low-fat minced meat • 1 tbsp olive oil • 2 carrots • ½ leek • 1 pinch of cinnamon • ½ tspn curry powder • salt, pepper

- Prepare the rice according to the instructions on the packaging.
- Peel the carrots and finely slice. Wash and clean the leek. Halve lengthways, then cut into quarters and then chop roughly.
- Heat the oil in a large pan. Stir-fry the minced meat until it has a nice brown color. Add the spices and fry for 1 to 2 minutes. Add the vegetables and stir-fry for 10 minutes. Season well with salt and pepper.
- Drain the rice well. Place the rice in the pan and stir carefully.

TIP: You can easily double the ingredients and freeze the rest!

Greek-Style Stir-Fry

For 2 servings:
1 red onion • 2 cloves of garlic • 1 carrot • 2 celery stalks • ½ lb ground beef • 1 tbsp olive oil • 1 tspn dried thyme • 1 tspn dried rosemary • 3 tbsp Worcestershire sauce • ½ bunch parsley

- Peel the onion and the garlic and finely chop. Peel the carrots and finely slice. Clean and wash the celery and finely chop.
- Place the ground beef in a hot pan and pull apart with a spatula. Season well with salt, pepper, thyme and olive oil. Stir-fry until the beef has a nice brown color.
- Add the rosemary, the garlic and the Worcestershire sauce. Fry until the beef looks shiny. Add the vegetables and put on a lid. Fry at a low heat until the vegetables are soft (this should take 5 to 10 minutes).
- Wash the parsley, shake dry and finely chop. Add to the beef. Serve hot.

TIPS: This is great with baked potatoes and green salad! If you can't eat onions and garlic: use a zucchini instead!

Chili con Carne

For 2 servings:
1 tbsp olive oil • 2 onions • ½ green bell pepper • ¾ lb minced meat • 1 can (15 oz) tomatoes • 1 can (15 oz) red beans • 1-2 tbsp chili spice (to taste) • baguette

- Peel the onions and finely chop. Deseed the bell pepper, wash and cut into strips.
- Heat the oil in a pot. Fry the onion until soft. Add the minced meat and the bell pepper and stir-fry for 5 minutes.
- Add the tomatoes and the beans (the entire can, not just the beans). Season with chili spice and stir well. Let the chili simmer for 10 minutes.
- Serve hot with baguette.

Fast Goulash

For 2 servings:
½ lb beef • 2 tbsp oil • 1 small onion • 1 green bell pepper • sugar, salt, pepper, hot paprika • 3 tomatoes • baguette

- Wash the beef and cut into bite-size pieces.
- Peel the onion and roughly chop. Deseed the bell pepper, wash and cut into strips.
- Heat the oil in a pot. Stir-fry the beef for 2 to 3 minutes. Add the onion and the bell pepper. Season well with sugar, salt, pepper, and paprika. Place the lid on the pot and let stew for 15 minutes.
- In the meantime, bring water to the boil in a small pot. Wash the tomatoes and make 2 cross cuts. Place in the boiling water for 1 to 2 minutes. Then remove the peel, cut into quarters and add to the goulash.
- Serve hot with baguette.

FISH STICKS WITH MASHED PEAS

For 1 serving:
5 fish sticks • 1 medium-size potato • ½ cup frozen peas • salt, pepper • 4 oz skim milk

To taste and tolerance:
a little fresh or dried mint

- Prepare the fish fingers in the oven according to the package instructions.
- Bring the water to the boil in a small pot.
- Peel the potatoes and cut into thin slices. Once boiling, place in the pot and cook for 10 minutes. Add the peas and the mint after 5 minutes.
- Drain the potatoes and the peas and put them back into the pot. Using a masher, roughly mash the potatoes and the peas. Stir in the milk and season well with salt and pepper. Serve hot with the fish fingers.

FISH BUNS WITH TARTAR SAUCE

For 2 buns:
4 fish sticks • 2 buns • 1 tomato • 1 red onion • a few lettuce leaves • 3 small pickled cucumbers • 5 oz low-fat natural yoghurt • ½ tspn mustard • 1 tspn dried dill • ketchup (to taste)

- Prepare the fish sticks and the buns according to the instructions on the packaging.
- Wash the tomato. Peel the onion. Cut both into slices.
- For the tartar sauce: cut the pickled cucumbers into small dice. Mix the yoghurt and the mustard. Add the cucumber dice and the dill and stir well.
- Place a lettuce leave on the bottom part of a bun. Add tomato and onion slices. Place 2 fish sticks on top and sprinkle with tartar sauce. Add ketchup to taste. Place the top half of the bun on top and serve immediately.

COUSCOUS WITH FENNEL AND SHRIMPS

For 1 serving:
8 tbsp couscous • 1 fennel • 7 oz shrimp (in brine, cooked) • ½ lemon • salt, pepper

To taste and tolerance:
1 tbsp olive oil • 2 tbsp low-fat natural yoghurt

- Prepare the couscous according to the instructions on the package.
- Trim the fennel. Cut the fennel into halve and remove the stem. Then finely slice the fennel.
- Drain the shrimps. Fluff up the couscous. Add the fennel and the shrimp. Season with lemon juice, salt and pepper. Toss well.
- Serve to taste with olive oil and yoghurt.

TIP: If your digestive system can't tolerate raw vegetables, you can fry the fennel in a little olive oil. Or, if you have one, use a steamer!

NEAPOLITAN COD

For 2 servings:
¾ lb cod fillets • 2 tspn lemon juice • salt, pepper • ½ lb tomatoes • 1 small onion • 1 clove of garlic • 1 tbsp olive oil • 1 tbsp tomato puree • 2 tbsp pitted green olives • 1 tspn capers • 1½ tspn each: dried basil, marjoram, thyme, rosemary • ciabatta bread, to serve

- Wash the fish fillets and pat dry. Drizzle the fish fillets with lemon juice and salt on both sides.
- Wash the tomatoes, cut in half, remove the stem and roughly chop. Peel the onion and the garlic and finely chop. Cut the olives into fine rings.
- Heat the oil in a pan. Once hot, stir-fry the onion and the garlic until transparent. Add the tomato puree. Add the chopped tomatoes. Add 5 fl oz of water and bring to a boil. Add the olives and the capers. Season well with dried herbs and salt and pepper.
- Place the fish fillets on the vegetables. Put on the lid and let it cook for 10 minutes.
- Serve hot with ciabatta bread.

Fish with couscous

For 2 servings:
2 fish fillet of frozen white fish (zander, plaice, etc.) • 5 oz frozen shrimps • lemon juice • ½ lb cherry tomatoes • 2 clove of garlic • 2 tbsp olive oil • salt, pepper • 8 tbsp couscous

- Preheat the oven to 400 °F.
- Place the frozen fish and shrimps in a baking dish. Drizzle with lemon juice.
- Peel the garlic and cut into fine slices. Wash the cherry tomatoes. Place the garlic and the tomatoes in the baking dish.
- Drizzle with olive oil and season well with salt and pepper. Place in the preheated oven and cook for 15 minutes.
- In the meantime, prepare the couscous according to the instructions on the package.
- Serve the fish hot with couscous.

French-style one-pan fish

For 2 servings:
¾ cup boil-in-the-bag rice • 2 small cod or rose fish fillets • 2 tspn lemon juice • 1 small zucchini • ½ eggplant • 1 large tomato • 2 tspn olive oil • 6 fl oz vegetable stock • herbes de provence • salt, pepper

- Prepare the rice according to the instructions on the package.
- Wash the fish fillets and pat dry. Drizzle the fish fillets with lemon juice and salt on both sides.
- Wash the zucchini, eggplant and tomato and roughly chop. Heat the oil in a pot. Once hot, stir-fry the vegetables for 4 to 5 minutes. Add the vegetable stock and season well with herbs and spices.
- Place the fish fillets on the vegetables. Put on the lid and let it cook for 10 minutes.
- Serve the fish hot together with the rice.

All rights reserved.

Publisher:
Iris Pilzer • Schärdinger Str. 50 • 94032 Passau • Germany • info@irispilzer.de

Photos:
Canva.com • Depositphotos.com

Disclaimer:
I'm neither a doctor nor a nutritionist. I tested all recipes and tips in this cookbook myself. But, as you know, people are different. This is why I can't guarantee that my recipes will work for you the way they worked for me. Food and diet is always trial and error. Think of this cookbook as a guide that helps you on your way to find the food you can eat without any problems.

Made in the USA
Columbia, SC
02 July 2021